Comptroller of the Currency
Administrator of National Banks

Analytical Review
of Income and Expense

Comptroller's Handbook
(Section 401)

Narrative - March 1990, Procedures - March 1998

E

Earnings

Analytical Review of Income and Expense (Section 401)

Table of Contents

Analytical Review of
Income and Expense
(Section 401)   Introduction

This section is designed to assist the examiner in developing an overview of the financial condition and results of operations of a bank through the use of analytical review techniques. It also provides procedures to assist in evaluating the reasonableness and reliability of the bank's income and expense accounts. A general understanding of a bank's balance sheet, income and expense accounts, and the Uniform Bank Performance Report (UBPR) is necessary to analyze a bank's earnings performance effectively. Therefore, the bank's Reports of Condition and Income and the UBPR should be reviewed prior to, or in conjunction with, the review of this area.

Overview

The review and analysis of the bank's financial condition and results of operations should begin during the initial review of the bank using the most recent UBPR. This review is meant to identify potential problem areas in order to properly scope the supervisory activity, ensure the availability of adequate staff resources, and select appropriate review procedures.

Questions raised during the initial review should be answered and substantiated soon after commencing the supervisory activity while performing the more comprehensive analytic review of bank earnings.

The analytic review will draw on various sources of information, other than the UBPR, the primary source. The major sources for earnings include the bank's financial statements and general ledger; income statement; financial budgets and underlying assumptions; Management Information System reports, both formal (reports to the board or senior management) and informal (committee reports); and call reports. Transaction journals and/or subsidiary ledgers may also provide reliable and detailed information if unusual conditions are identified during the review. Work performed to substantiate explanations of unusual items should be documented in the working papers.

In some cases, selected review and verification procedures for income and expense accounts may be performed by examiners assigned to other areas of the supervisory activity. For example, interest income may be verified by procedures described in the various loan sections or in "Investment Securities"; depreciation expense and repairs and maintenance expense may be tested in "Bank Premises and Equipment"; interest expense and service charge income may be tested under "Deposit Accounts"; or, interest expense associated with borrowed funds may be tested under "Borrowed Funds." For income and expense accounts not tested elsewhere by other examining personnel or by the bank's internal or external auditors, the examiner may wish to perform the verification procedures described in this section.

Analytic Review

Analytic review involves a comparison of detail balances or statistical data on a period-to-period basis in an effort to substantiate reasonableness without systematic examination of the transactions comprising the account balances. Analytic review is based on the assumption that comparability of period- to-period balances and ratios shows them to be free from significant error. A well-performed analytic review not only benefits the examination by providing an understanding of the bank's operations, but also highlights matters of interest and potential problem situations which, if detected early, might avert more serious problems.

The basic analysis tools available to the examiner are UBPR and the financial statements of the bank. Internally prepared statements and supplemental schedules, if available, are excellent supplements to an in-depth analytic review. The information from those schedules may give the examiner considerable insight into the interpretation of the bank's basic financial statements. Internally prepared information is not in itself sufficient to adequately analyze the financial condition of the bank. To properly understand and interpret financial and statistical data, the examiner should be familiar with current economic conditions and any secular, cyclical, or seasonal factors, nationally, regionally, and locally, including general industry conditions. Maintaining a current knowledge of such conditions and factors by reviewing appropriate economic and industry information, Office of the Comptroller of the Currency (OCC) releases and reports and industry journals is important to the examiner in adequately reviewing and analyzing a bank.

An analytic review of a bank's financial statements requires professional judgment, imagination, and discrimination as well as an inquiring attitude. The examiner should, during such an analysis, avoid details that may not specifically relate to his or her objective. It is important to maintain a sense of proportion when analyzing the statements and to avoid spending excessive time on relatively immaterial amounts.

It is generally more efficient to review financial data that has been rounded to the nearest thousand. Undue precision in computing and reviewing ratios should be avoided. An evaluation of the meaning of the ratios and amounts being compared is important and little can be gained by computing ratios for totally unrelated items. When comparing data on the bank under review to peer group data, the examiner should consider whether the bank is typical in its peer group (group of banks of similar size and reporting characteristics). For example, the bank might be of comparable size but, atypically, have earning assets comprised principally of agricultural loans or mortgage loans.

Alternative accounting treatments for similar transactions also should be considered because they may produce significantly different results. Consistency within a bank in the application of alternatives is important. Accordingly, during the analytical review, the examiner should determine any material inconsistency in the application of accounting principles.

One tool available to the examiner for analytic review is the UBPR, which is continually performed and updated. The reports display the results of various ratio calculations for a bank and its peer group for both current and prior periods. They also include summarized comparative financial statements for several periods.

The primary sources of information used to prepare UBPRs are the regularly filed statements of condition and reports of income. In certain circumstances, the examiner may be interested in a more detailed and current review of the bank than provided by the UBPR. For example, such circumstances occur because:

- Volume information, such as number of demand deposits, certificates of deposit, and other accounts, is not reported, and vulnerability in a bank subject to concentrations normally should be considered.

- Components of interest and fees on loans are not reported separately by category of loan; thus, adverse trends in the loan portfolio may not be detected. For example, the yield of a particular bank's loan portfolio may be similar to those of its peer group, but the examiner, by analytically scanning the income ledger cards, may detect an upward trend in yields for a specific category of loans. That upward trend might be partially or wholly offset by a downward trend of yields in another category of loans, and, although the bank may still be sound, the examiner should consider further investigating the circumstances applicable to each of those loan categories. OCC management might also request analyses of that type because of a changed circumstance detected by a financial analyst.

- Income or expense generated by new business or operations is not differentiated from that resulting from operations in existence for some time in the regularly filed financial information. When there has been a significant expansion activity, the examiner may wish to analyze its potential impact on future bank operations.

- Line items may appear insignificant, but the review of "netted" component figures may reveal matters needing further investigation. For example, security gains are netted against security losses. The net amount reported could be small and superficially unimportant. Each component amount, however, could be extremely large, and the examiner may need to ascertain the reasons for, and nature of, these transactions.

- The examiner should always be alert for irregular or unusual activity that may indicate possible fraud or illegal activity by insiders.

The UBPR is a valuable tool that may have to be supplemented with more in-depth analysis for the examiner to achieve an understanding of the quality and consistency of bank earnings.

After the examiner has completed the analytic review of the bank, he or she should have an understanding of its financial position and results of operations, and that understanding should make a substantial contribution to the timely and successful completion of the supervisory activity.

Analytical Review of
Income and Expense
(Section 401)

General Procedures

Some steps in these examination procedures require gathering information from or reviewing information with examiners in other areas. For example, examiners may want to discuss Deferred Income Taxes with examiners assigned Other Assets/Other Liabilities and Capital Accounts and Dividends or discuss Fiduciary earnings with examiners experienced in fiduciary matters. The examiner performing a review of income and expense should discuss such areas with the other examiners to avoid duplication of effort. The examiner should obtain information not available from other examiners directly from the bank. The availability of information will vary with the size and complexity of the bank. Where appropriate, the examiner should cross-reference working papers with other examination sections. As always, the examiner-in-charge must make the final decision on the examination's scope and how best to obtain needed information from the bank.

Objective: Determine the scope of the examination of Income and Expense.

1. Review the following documents to identify any previous problems that require follow-up:

    ☐ Supervisory strategy and most recent quarterly review in the OCC's electronic information system.
    ☐ EIC's scope memorandum including examination objectives for fiduciary earnings.
    ☐ Prior Report of Examination.
    ☐ Prior examination working papers.
    ☐ Correspondence.
    ☐ Management's responses.

2. Obtain from the examiner assigned Internal/External Audit a copy of any significant audit deficiencies for this area and determine if the bank has taken appropriate corrective action.

3. If the bank's total assets exceed $500 million, obtain a copy of the External Audit firm's report on the adequacy of internal controls (required by FDICIA) as it relates to this area.

4. If Internal/External Audit is not part of the overall scope of the examination, review the work performed by internal/external auditors as it relates to this area.

5. Obtain the following reports to identify trends in earnings performance:

   ☐ Uniform Bank Performance Report (UBPR).
   ☐ Bank Expert (BERT).
   ☐ The most recent annual report.
   ☐ Annual Report of Trust Assets.
   ☐ Regulatory reports (e.g., 10K, 10Q, Y9)

6. Obtain any reports management and the board of directors use to supervise financial performance to determine that they receive adequate information to assess earnings performance. Consider:

   ☐ Balance sheet and income statement.
   ☐ Budget and variance analysis.
   ☐ Strategic plan.
   ☐ Reports on deferred income taxes.
   ☐ Reports filed with the OCC pursuant to 12 CFR 11.
   ☐ Reports used to evaluate fiduciary earnings:
       – Fiduciary income statement;
       – Fiduciary budget and variance analysis;
       – Litigation reserves/estimates;
       – Charge-offs, recoveries, and fee offsets for the prior year and year to date.

7. Determine, during early discussions with management:

   • How management administers financial performance.
   • Any significant changes in the following:
       – Policies, practices, personnel.
       – Operations, including new services or substantially increased

volume of an activity or service.
  – Accounting practices or records.
  – Financial reporting.
  – General business conditions.
- Any other internal or external factors that could affect financial performance.

8.   Based on performance of the previous steps, combined with discussions with the bank EIC and other appropriate OCC supervisory personnel, confirm that the scope and objectives of the examination provided by the bank EIC are appropriate.

Select steps necessary to meet examination objectives from among the following examination procedures. All steps are seldom required in an examination.

Quantity of Risk

Conclusion: The quantity of risk is (low, moderate, high).

Objective: Determine the composition and quality of earnings given the size, complexity, and risk profile of the institution.

Composition of Earnings

1. Analyze the composition and trends in the bank's assets and liabilities to assess the impact on bank earnings. Refer to the Uniform Bank Performance Report (UBPR), Bank Expert (BERT), QCALC, Annual Report of Trust Assets, the company's annual report, and any other applicable management reports.

    During your analysis consider the following:

    *   Why significant growth or shrinkage occurred in major asset and liability categories over the past year and/or quarter (e.g. acquisitions).
    *   Whether asset or liability categories reflect new products or services (e.g., data processing, credit cards).
    *   How off balance sheet asset and liabilities contribute to the earnings' profile (e.g., derivatives).

2. Analyze the components of key earnings measures and trends over several periods. Some examples include:

    *   Return on average assets.
        *   How has the bank's tax position impacted its ROAA?
        *   Have any extraordinary gains or losses occurred?
        *   Has the bank realized gains or losses on its held-to-maturity and/or available-for-sale portfolios?

    *   The spread between interest earned and interest paid.
        *   What is the impact of deposit and loan pricing strategies?
        *   What changes have occurred in the bank's yields and cost of funds?

- Net interest margin.
  - Has the level of earning assets significantly changed?
  - Do net interest margin trends reflect volatility?

- Loan loss provisions and allocated transfer reserves ratios.
  - How does the trend in loan losses potentially impact the need for additional provisions?
  - Have the transfer reserve requirements for the bank's specific international assets changed?

- Operating Efficiency Ratios.
  - Is the ratio of operating expenses to operating revenues increasing?

- One way of further defining this efficiency ratio is to compute the following: Operating expenses (excluding interest expenses, amortization of purchased intangibles, OREO expenses, and Allowance for Loan and Lease Losses (ALLL) provisions) divided by operating income (net interest income and recurring non-interest income).
  - How do the bank's product lines (i.e., fee-based) impact its operating efficiency?
  - How do the bank's overhead expenses compare to those of peer banks?

Quality of Earnings

1. Review the level and trends of earnings from the bank's core activities. These will vary by bank. Consider the following:

    - The level and trend of interest income from loans, investments, and other assets.

    - The level, trend, and reliance of non-interest income from fiduciary, trading, and other fee-based activities. Note income from new activities.
      - For fiduciary activities, perform trend analysis of fiduciary income and expense items, as well as product mix, using financial statements for the current period and the previous five years. (Note: This procedure should use the analysis performed at the last examination. The examiner should not request five years worth of financial information at each examination.)

Consider:
- The method used to develop fee schedules.
- Fees charged to high-risk or high- cost accounts.
- Financial planning process and strategic goals.
- Actual earnings performance compared to budget.
- Income and expense allocation process, both within the bank and among affiliates.
- Significant losses, charge-offs, fee waivers, settlements, or other compromise actions.
- Accuracy of data contained in Schedule E of the Annual Report of Trust Assets.

2. Review the level, trends, and reliance of earnings from non-recurring sources. These also will vary by bank. Consider the following:

- Security gains.
- Cost reductions (e.g., staffing).
- Extraordinary items (e.g., litigation settlements).

3. Review the level and trend of interest expenses. Consider the following:

- Core and non-core deposit pricing.
- Short term and long-term borrowing costs.

4. Review the level and trend of non-interest expenses. Consider the following:

- Overhead expenses.
  - Does the bank's compensation plan include incentives that have significantly increased?
  - Have changes in the bank's occupancy expense changed? (e.g., new offices, renegotiated leases)

- Fees paid for professional services.
  - Does the bank pay a management fee to the parent company?
  - Has the level of legal fees significantly changed?
  - Has the amount of fees paid for accounting, audit, and compliance services significantly changed?

5. Discuss conclusions with examiners responsible for other areas of the examination to determine the impact on earnings. Consider:

    - Consulting with the EIC to determine the earnings needs for new product lines.
    - Consulting with the examiner evaluating Capital Accounts and Dividends to determine the need for earnings to support debt service at the bank or holding company level.
    - Consulting with the examiner evaluating the ALLL and other valuation allowance accounts to determine the need for additional provisions or transfers.
    - Consulting with the examiner evaluating Funds Management to determine earnings' exposure to market risk such as interest rate, foreign currency translation, and price risks.
    - Consulting with the examiner assigned review of Regulatory Reports to ascertain whether adjustments to the Reports of Condition and Income will result in restating earnings for a previous period.

6. As appropriate, adjust the bank's reported earnings to reflect the results of the examination and to project current year's net income. Distribute adjustments to appropriate examining personnel.

Objective: Determine compliance with appropriate laws and regulations and conformance to established accounting rules.

1. Through discussions with other examiners, determine compliance with 12 USC 161—Reports to the Comptroller of the Currency, Report of Condition.

2. If applicable, review the bank's adherence to FAS 91, "Accounting for Nonrefundable Fees and Costs Associated with Originating or Acquiring Loans and Initial Direct Costs of Leases."

3. If the bank has capitalized computer software costs developed for others, review the bank's adherence to FAS 86, "Accounting for the Costs of Computer Software to be Sold, Leased, or Otherwise Marketed"

4. Review any other applicable accounting issuances.

Quality of Risk Management

Conclusion: The quality of risk management is (strong, satisfactory, weak).

Policy

Conclusion: The Board (has/has not) established financial performance guidelines consistent with business and operational risks.

Objective: Determine the board's financial performance guidelines.

1. Determine if lines of authority and responsibility are established.

2. Determine if formal or informal financial performance policies have been established and approved by managerial personnel and/or the board of directors, as applicable. Consider:

    -   Strategic planning.
    -   Budget goals.
    -   Income/expense forecasts for:
        -   Nontraditional income sources, fee income, trading, etc.
        -   Fiduciary income.

3. Determine if the board has adopted proper accounting, audit and internal control policies governing income and expense areas to effectively manage risk. Consider whether these formal or informal policies impact the bank's capacity to operate in a safe and sound manner.

Processes

Conclusion: Management and the Board have (effective/ineffective) processes and procedures to manage and monitor earnings performance.

Objective: Determine the adequacy of the bank's planning and budgeting processes.

1. Obtain and review the following reports prior to meeting with management to discuss the bank's planning process:

☐ Profit plans.
☐ Budgets.
☐ Mid- and long-range financial plans.
☐ Variance reports.
☐ Any related progress reports.
☐ Economic advisory reports.

2. Determine if earnings projections and objectives are reasonable. Consider:

    • Actual earnings results to budgeted amounts over the past year.
    • How the bank's short term and long term goals have impacted earnings (e.g., growth plans).
    • The frequency of planning revisions.
    • What triggers a specific plan revision.
    • Who initiates plan revisions.
    • Whether the bank requires explanations for significant variations in balance sheet and income and expense accounts.
    • Whether the bank determines the cause of variations before implementing corrective action such as adjustments to strategies, revised goals, etc.
    • The sources of input for forecasts, plans, and budgets.

3. Discuss with trust management the method used to establish the trust fee schedules. Consider:

    • The impact of competition on the fee schedules.
    • Whether management adjusts the fee charged to high-risk or high-cost accounts.

Objective: Determine if accounting and internal control procedures relating to income and expense are sufficient.

1. Research the cause of any significant accounting errors or adjusting entries to income and expense accounts noted by the bank's auditors or continual amendments to the bank's call reports. Determine that management effectively implemented corrective action.

2.   Scan ledger accounts entries for unusual items and significant fluctuations as necessary and discuss unusual entries and significant fluctuations with bank management. Consider:

- Significant deviations from the normal amounts of recurring entries.
- Unusual debit entries in income accounts or unusual credit entries in expense accounts (e.g. trust income and expense accounts).
- Significant entries from an unusual source, such as a journal entry.
- Significant entries in "other income" or "other expense" which may indicate fee or service losses on an off-balance sheet activity (e.g., derivatives, financial advisory or underwriting services).
- Instances of diversion of bank income to enhance another unit's profit.
- Charges that do not represent justified bank expenses.
- Unpaid invoices. If a bill exceeds 30 days and has not been reflected in a bookkeeping entry (recorded as an account payable and expense), investigate why.

3.   Determine the reason for any outdated and/or unusual items. As appropriate, request charge-off or reversal of stale items.

4.   Determine that accounts including accrued expenses and taxes are reconciled and documented on a regular basis.

5.   Determine whether the deferred tax accounts reconcile for the current period.

- Obtain the bank's prior year-end deferred tax liability (asset) account balance from call report Schedule RC-G (RC-F). Add the deferred tax expense (or benefit) for the current year as reported on Schedule RI-C to the prior year-end deferred tax liability (or asset) account balance.

- Based on the schedules reviewed above, determine if the resulting balance agrees with the bank's deferred tax liability (or asset) balance as reported at the current year-end financial statements.

Objective: Determine if internal control procedures and segregation of duties are adequate.

General Ledger Entries

1.   Review the internal control procedures in place for general ledger entries. Consider:

- Is the general ledger posted daily?
- Is a daily statement of condition prepared?
- Are the general books of the bank maintained by someone who does not have access to cash?
- Are all general ledger entries approved by a responsible person other than the general ledger bookkeeper or person associated with its preparation?
- Are corrections to ledgers made by posting a correcting entry and not by erasing (manual process) or deleting (computerized system) the incorrect entry?
- Is there a process to communicate changes in accounting policies, especially those resulting from generally accepted accounting principles (GAAP) and regulatory accounting principles (RAP)?

Purchasing

1.   Review the internal control procedures in place for purchasing. Consider the following:

- If the bank has a separate purchasing department, is it independent of the accounting and receiving departments?
- Are purchases made only when requisitions are signed by authorized persons?
- Are all purchases routed through a purchasing department or personnel functioning in that capacity?
- Are all purchases made by means of pre-numbered purchase orders sent to vendors?
- Are all invoices received checked against purchase orders and receiving department reports?
- Are all invoices tested for clerical accuracy?
- Are invoice amounts credited to their respective accounts and tested periodically for accuracy?

Disbursements

1.   Review the internal control procedures for disbursements. Consider the following:

- Is payment for all purchases, except minor items, made by official check?
- Does the official signing the check review all supporting documents?
- Are supporting vouchers and invoices canceled to prevent reuse?
- Are duties and responsibilities in the following areas segregated?
  - Authorization to issue expense checks?
  - Preparation of expense checks?
  - Signing of expense checks?
  - Sending of expense checks?
  - Use and storage of facsimile signatures?
  - General ledger posting?
  - Subsidiary ledger posting?

Payroll

1. Review the internal control procedures for payroll systems. Consider the following:

    - Is the payroll department separate from the personnel department?
    - Are signed authorizations on file for all payroll deductions, including W-4 forms for withholding?
    - Are salaries authorized by the board of directors or its designated committee?
    - Are individual wage rates authorized in writing by an authorized officer?
    - Are vacation and sick leave payments fixed and authorized?
    - Are payrolls paid from a special bank account or directly credited to the employee's demand deposit account?
    - Are time records reviewed and signed by the employee's supervisor?
    - Are hours, rates, deductions, extensions, and footings checked and verified at least twice before posting?
    - Are payroll signers independent of the persons approving hours worked and persons preparing the payroll?
    - If a check-signing machine is used, are controls over its use adequate (such as dual control)?
    - Does a bank officer give payrolls final approval?
    - Are the names of persons leaving the bank's employment reported promptly in writing to the payroll department?
    - Are payroll expense distributions reconciled with the general payroll payment records?

Personnel

Conclusion: Given the size and complexity of the bank, management personnel (do/do not) possess the required technical skills and knowledge to perform financial management duties.

Objective: Determine the competence of bank managers/personnel performing financial management duties.

1. Assess bank managers and staff's knowledge and technical skills related to financial performance based on conclusions developed while performing these procedures. Consider:

   - Expertise in strategic planning, accounting, taxes, and financial reporting, as applicable.
   - Work experience.
   - Professional designations (i.e., CPA).
   - Continuing education programs.

Controls

Conclusion: Given the size and complexity of the bank, management (has/has not) established effective control systems for income and expense areas.

Objective: Determine whether control systems are appropriate and effective.

1. Determine if internal controls and information systems are adequately tested and reviewed. Consider the following:

   - Are risk measurement tools accurate, independent, and reliable?
   - Is the frequency of testing adequate given the level of risk and sophistication of risk management decisions?
   - Are reports prepared that provide key information?
   - Do periodic reports identify and comment on major changes in risk profiles?

2. Determine if audit findings and management responses to those findings are sufficiently documented and tracked for adequate follow-up.

3. Review a sample of recent audit findings and determine whether follow-up was completed in a timely manner. If not, determine why.

4. Determine if management gives identified material weaknesses appropriate and

timely attention. Consider:

- Management's record of completing corrective action to correct identified weaknesses.
- Have actions taken by management to deal with material weaknesses been verified and reviewed for objectivity and adequacy by senior management or the board?
- Whether line management is held accountable for unsatisfactory or ineffective follow-up.
- Whether unusual entries or significant fluctuations in income and expense accounts were adequately researched and explained.

Objective: Determine whether management information systems provide accurate and comprehensive information for assessing financial performance.

1. Evaluate periodic earnings reports to determine that management and the board of directors receive adequate information to assess earnings performance. Consider:

    - Rationale for adjustments made to management reports for financial performance.
    - The account detail provided to management for analyzing fluctuations and the capabilities of expanding the detail if requested by management or the Board.
    - The availability of financial performance reports for the parent company as well as major units of the bank.

Conclusion

Objective: To finalize and communicate examination findings and appropriate corrective action.

1. Determine the CAMELS Earnings component rating using OCC 97-1 as guidance. Consider:

    - The level of earnings, including trends and stability.
    - The ability to provide for adequate capital through retained earnings.
    - The quality and sources of earnings.
    - The level of expenses in relation to operations.
    - The adequacy of budgeting systems, forecasting processes, and management information systems in general.
    - The adequacy of provisions to maintain the allowance for loan and lease losses and other valuation allowance accounts.

2. Determine the Fiduciary Earnings component rating. Consider:

    - The level and consistency of profitability.
    - Dependence on non-recurring fees and commissions.
    - Unusual features regarding the composition of business, fee schedules and effects of charge-offs and compromise action.
    - Methods of allocating income and expense within the bank and among affiliates.
    - Management's use of budgets, projections and other cost analysis procedures.
    - New business development efforts.

3. Determine the impact on the aggregate and direction of risk assessments from any applicable risks identified by performing the above procedures. Examiners should refer to guidance provided under the OCC's large and community bank risk assessment programs. Consider:

    - Risk Categories: Compliance, Credit, Foreign Currency Translation, Interest Rate, Liquidity, Price, Reputation, Strategic, Transaction
    - Risk Conclusions: High, Moderate, or Low
    - Risk Direction: Increasing, Stable, or Decreasing

For banks with an Earnings component rating of 1 or 2, perform the following procedures:

1. Provide the EIC with brief conclusions. Consider:

    - Recommended earnings component rating.
    - Recommended Fiduciary earnings component rating, if applicable.
    - Quantity of risk.
    - Quality of risk management.
    - Any concerns and/or recommendations.

2. Determine in consultation with EIC, if the risks identified are significant enough to merit bringing them to the board's attention in the Report of Examination. If so, prepare items for inclusion under the heading Matters Requiring Board Attention (MRBA).

    - MRBA should cover practices that:
      - Deviate from sound fundamental principles and are likely to result in financial deterioration if not addressed.
      - Result in substantive noncompliance with laws.

    - MRBA should discuss:
      - Causative factors contributing to the problem.
      - Consequences of inaction.
      - Management's commitment for corrective action.
      - The time frame and person(s) responsible for corrective.

3. Discuss findings with management, including conclusions regarding applicable risks. Consider:

    - Recommended earnings component rating.
    - Recommended fiduciary earnings component rating, if applicable.
    - Deficiencies in, and deviations from, policies, practices, procedures, and internal controls.
    - Violations of law, rulings, or regulations, with particular focus and emphasis on the causes.
    - Composition of earnings and trends.
    - Any UBPR peer group data that should be brought to the attention of

management.
- Adequacy of earnings to support present and planned activities.
- Ability of earnings to meet dividend projections.
- Earnings capacity to cover losses and provide for adequate capital.
- Reliance on unusual, extraordinary items, or nonrecurring gains or losses.
- Adequacy of net interest margin.
- Accuracy and comprehensiveness of management information systems.

4. Prepare a brief earnings comment for inclusion in the Report of Examination. Consider:

- Earnings ratings (CAMELS, UITRS).
- Quantity of risk.
- Quality of risk management.
- The level and sustainability of earnings, including fiduciary earnings.
- Adequacy of policies, processes, personnel and control systems.
- Any deficiencies reviewed with management and any corrective actions recommended.

5. Update the OCC's electronic information system and any applicable Report of Examination schedule or table.

6. Distribute findings to other examination areas as appropriate.

7. Organize and reference working papers in accordance with OCC guidance. Document in the working papers your decision on required follow-up.

For banks with an Earnings component rating of 3 or worse, complete the following procedures:

1. Provide the EIC with a detailed conclusion comment. Consider:

- Recommended earnings component rating.
- Recommended Fiduciary earnings component rating, if applicable.
- Quantity of risk.
- Quality of risk management.

- Concerns and recommendations.
  - What are the root causes of the problems?
  - What factors contributed to the less than satisfactory conditions?
- Ability of management to correct noted deficiencies.

2.   Develop, in consultation with the EIC, a strategy to address the bank's weaknesses and discuss the strategy with the appropriate supervisory office or manager.

3.   Determine in consultation with EIC, which of the risks identified are significant enough to merit bringing them to the board's attention in the Report of Examination. Prepare items for inclusion under the heading Matters Requiring Board Attention. Consider:

- MRBA should cover practices that:
  - Deviate from sound fundamental principles and are likely to result in financial deterioration if not addressed.
  - Result in substantive noncompliance with laws.

- MRBA should discuss:
  - Causative factors contributing to the problem.
  - Consequences of inaction.
  - Management's commitment for corrective action.
  - The time frame and person(s) responsible for corrective action.

4.   Discuss findings, including conclusions on applicable risks with senior management. Consider:

- Recommended earnings component rating.
- Recommended fiduciary earnings component rating, if applicable.
- Deficiencies in, and deviations from, policies, practices, procedures, and internal controls.
- Violations of law, rulings, or regulations, with particular focus and emphasis on the causes.
- Composition of earnings and trends, particularly any adverse trends.
- Any UBPR peer group data that should be brought to the attention of management.
- Adequacy of earnings to support present and planned activities.
- Ability of earnings to meet dividend projections.
- Earnings capacity to cover losses and provide for adequate capital.

- Reliance on unusual, extraordinary items, or nonrecurring gains or losses.
- Adequacy of net interest margin.
- Accuracy and comprehensiveness of management information systems.

5. Prepare an earnings comment for inclusion in the Report of Examination. Consider:

- Earnings ratings (CAMELS, UITRS).
- Quantity of risk.
- Quality of risk management.
- The level and sustainability of earnings, including fiduciary earnings.
- Adequacy of policies, processes, personnel and control systems.
- Deficiencies reviewed with management and any corrective actions recommended.

6. Update the OCC's electronic information system and any applicable Report of Examination schedule or table.

7. Distribute findings to other examination areas as appropriate.

8. Organize and reference working papers in accordance with OCC guidance. Document in the working papers your decision on required follow-up.